201 drinks for health & vitality

JUICES
AND
SMOOTHIES

AMANDA CROSS, PENNY HUNKING,
FIONA HUNTER & CHARMAINE YABSLEY

HAMLYN HEALTHY EATING

An Hachette UK Company
www.hachette.co.uk

First published in Great Britain in 2003 by Hamlyn,
a division of Octopus Publishing Group Ltd
Endeavour House
189 Shaftesbury Avenue
London
WC2H 8JY
www.octopusbooksusa.com

Revised edition 2008
This edition published in 2014

Distributed in the US by
Hachette Book Group USA
237 Park Avenue
New York NY 10017 USA

Distributed in Canada by
Canadian Manda Group
165 Dufferin Street
Toronto, Ontario, Canada M6K 3H6

This material was previously published in *Miracle Juices*
and *Power Juices*.

ISBN 978-0-600-62976-4

Printed and bound in China

10 9 8 7 6 5 4 3 2 1

All the recipes in this book have been tested using the
Oscar Pulverizing Juicer.
If a different juicer is used the quantity of juice may vary.

contents

Introduction

Ask many people what would improve their quality of life, and it is likely that "more energy" would feature prominently among their answers. We are all aware that food is our main source of energy, and that we should "eat five" (eat five portions of fruit or vegetables) each day, but many of us don't. Instead, knowingly or otherwise, we undermine the value of food by eating too much of the wrong kinds, and too little of the right kinds, not to mention skipping meals altogether. Homemade juices and smoothies are a simple, delicious, and relatively inexpensive way to keep up our intake of the good guys, boosting energy levels, and aiding a general feeling of wellbeing along the way.

What's so great about juices and smoothies?

Fruit and vegetables contain many of the important enzymes, vitamins, and minerals that we need to stay healthy, be full of energy, and fight off disease. Juicing several types of raw fruits and vegetables daily is an easy—not to mention tasty—way to ensure you receive your full quota of these vital nutrients. Juices contain no fiber or pulp because liquid from the fruit or vegetable is extracted by pressing or squeezing with great force, and discarding any residual pulp. As the juice contains all of the goodness but no hard-to-digest fiber, the nutrients are readily absorbed by the body for almost instant use. Smoothies are thicker and more pulpy as they are a mixture of freshly squeezed juice and some of the crushed fruit, and may also contain other ingredients such as milk or yogurt.

Eat well, look great

All this goodness on the inside will have a positive effect on the outside because feeling fit, healthy, and energized really shows. Take antioxidants, for example. They are present in fruits and vegetables and are essential to a younger-looking skin. Also present in many fruits and vegetables is folic acid, which helps to keep hair and nails strong.

Another advantage of drinking juices and smoothies is that they automatically up our intake of water. It is easy to forget to drink enough water and so much of what we drink (tea, coffee, flavored drinks and alcohol) contains substances that are in themselves dehydrating, but fruit and vegetable juices are not.

Don't forget

Juices and smoothies should be used as part of a sensible eating plan so you must still eat enough from the other food groups (such as grains, dairy foods, and pulses). If you are following a special diet, or are under medical supervision, consult your health practitioner before making drastic changes to your health regime.

smooth operator

apple and blueberry smoothie

bugsy banana

banana and peanut butter smoothie

1 ripe banana
1¼ cups lowfat milk
**1 tablespoon smooth peanut butter or
  2 teaspoons tahini paste**

Peel and slice the banana and freeze for at least 2 hours or overnight. Put the banana, milk, and peanut butter or tahini paste in a blender, and process until smooth.

Makes about 1½ cups

rocket fuel

1 ripe mango
1¼ cups pineapple juice
rind and juice of ½ lime

Roughly chop the mango flesh and freeze for at least 2 hours or overnight. Place the frozen mango in a blender with the pineapple juice, lime rind and juice, and process until thick. Decorate with lime wedges, if desired.

Makes about 1½ cups

maybe baby

1 pear
½ avocado

Juice the pear, and then blend it with the avocado. Pour into a glass, and add a couple of ice cubes.

Makes about ⅔ cup

high flyer

1 ripe mango
¾ cup cranberry juice
⅔ cup peach yogurt

Roughly chop the mango flesh and place in a blender with the cranberry juice and yogurt. Process until smooth and pour into a glass. Add a couple of ice cubes and decorate with fresh cranberries, if desired.

Makes about 1½ cups

rocket fuel

high flyer

round the clock

I small ripe avocado
I small ripe banana
I cup skim milk

Roughly chop the avocado flesh and slice the banana. Place with the milk in a blender and process to make a high-energy smoothie. Pour into a glass, and add a couple of ice cubes.

Makes about 1½ cups

prune, apple, and cinnamon smoothie

¾ cup ready-to-eat prunes
pinch of ground cinnamon
1⅓ cups apple juice
3 tablespoons Greek yogurt

Roughly chop the prunes and place with the cinnamon in a large bowl. Pour over the apple juice, cover and let stand overnight. Place the prune and apple juice mixture with the yogurt in a blender and process until smooth. Pour into a glass, add ice cubes, and sprinkle with cinnamon, if desired.

Makes about 1½ cups

jumping jack

2 very ripe bananas
1⅔ cups soy milk
¼ cup ground almonds
pinch of ground cinnamon
a little honey (optional)

Slice the bananas and freeze for at least 2 hours or overnight. Place the frozen bananas, soy milk, ground almonds, and cinnamon in a blender. Add the honey, if using, and process until thick and frothy. Pour into glasses, add a couple of ice cubes, and decorate with ground cinnamon, if desired.

Makes about 2½ cups

summer berry smoothie

¾ cup frozen mixed summer berries
1¼ cups vanilla-flavored soy milk
I teaspoon clear honey (optional)

Place the berries, soy milk, and honey, if using, in a blender and process until thick. Serve immediately, decorated with berries if desired.

Makes about 1½ cups

round the clock

jumping jack

summer berry smoothie

peach and orange smoothie

13 oz can peaches in natural juice, drained
⅔ cup peach or apricot yogurt
¾ cup orange juice
a little honey (optional)

Place the peaches in a blender with the yogurt, orange juice, and honey, if using, and process until smooth. Add a couple of ice cubes, and decorate with slices of peach, if desired.

Makes about 2 cups

rhubarb and custard smoothie

5 oz can rhubarb
⅔ cup store-bought custard
⅓ cup lowfat milk, ice-cold
I teaspoon confectioners' sugar (optional)

Drain the rhubarb, then put it into a blender with the custard, milk, and confectioners' sugar, if using, and process until smooth. Pour into a glass, and add a couple of ice cubes, if desired.

Makes about 1½ cups

all nighter

I small ripe banana
⅓ cup strawberries, hulled
I cup orange juice

Slice the banana and roughly chop the strawberries. Freeze the fruit for at least 2 hours or overnight. Place the frozen fruit and the orange juice in a blender and process until thick. Decorate with strawberries, if desired.

Makes about 1½ cups

big boost

½ cup dried apricots
1⅓ cups pineapple juice

Roughly chop the apricots into small pieces and put them in a large bowl. Pour the pineapple juice over them, cover the bowl, and let stand overnight. Tip the contents into a blender and process until smooth. Serve in a glass with a couple of ice cubes, if desired.

Makes about 1½ cups

peach and orange smoothie

all nighter

big boost

banana and mango smoothie

I ripe banana
I ripe mango
¾ cup orange juice
¾ cup lowfat milk
3 tablespoons fromage frais

Slice the banana and roughly chop the mango flesh. Put with the orange juice, milk, and fromage frais into a blender and process until smooth. Pour into a glass and add a couple of ice cubes to chill.

Makes about 2 cups

blackberry and grape smoothie

¼ lb frozen blackberries
I ¼ cups purple grape juice
3 tablespoons quark or fromage frais
I teaspoon clear honey (optional)

Put the blackberries, grape juice, and quark or fromage frais in a food processor or blender. Add the honey, if using, and process until thick. Decorate with blackberries, if desired.

Makes about I ⅓ cups

apple pie

⅓ cup apple juice
⅓ cup store-bought custard
ground cinnamon, to taste

Blend the ice-cold apple juice and custard until smooth, then serve sprinkled with cinnamon.

Makes about ¾ cup

fruit smoothie

I papaya
I orange
I banana
I ¼ cups apple juice

Halve and seed the papaya. Scoop out the flesh, cut the orange into segments, and whizz together with the chopped banana in a blender. Add the mixture to the apple juice and stir well. Serve with ice, if desired.

Makes about I ½ cups

apple pie

blackberry and grape smoothie

fruit smoothie

kiwifruit, melon, and passion fruit smoothie

¼ watermelon, about ½–¾ lb flesh
2 kiwifruit
¾ cup passion fruit juice

Remove and discard the seeds from the watermelon and dice the flesh. Freeze for at least 2 hours or overnight. Peel and roughly chop the kiwifruit and place them in a blender with the watermelon and passion fruit juice and process until thick. Decorate with passion fruit seeds, if desired.

Makes about 1½ cups

quick hit

¼ lb strawberries, hulled
1 small ripe mango
1¼ cups orange juice

Roughly chop the strawberries and the mango flesh and freeze for at least 2 hours or overnight. Place them in a blender with the orange juice and process until thick. Decorate with slices of mango, if desired.

Makes about 1½ cups

strawberry and pineapple smoothie

¾ cup strawberries, hulled
⅔ cup pineapple juice
⅔ cup strawberry yogurt

Roughly chop the strawberries, and freeze for at least 2 hours or overnight. Place the frozen strawberries, pineapple juice, and yogurt in a blender and process until smooth. Pour into a glass. Add a couple of ice cubes, and decorate with strawberries, if desired.

Makes about 1½ cups

bionic tonic

1 large banana
1 large ripe mango
⅔ cup natural bio yogurt
1¼ cups pineapple juice

Slice the banana and roughly chop the mango flesh. Freeze for at least 2 hours or overnight. Place the frozen banana and mango in a blender with the yogurt and pineapple juice. Process until smooth. Serve in a glass and decorate with pineapple chunks, if desired.

Makes about 2½ cups

quick hit

kiwifruit, melon, and passion fruit smoothie

bionic tonic

sleeping beauty

¾ cup soy milk
2 kiwifruit
⅔ cup fresh or frozen strawberries, hulled
¼ cup slivered almonds

Put all the ingredients in a food processor or blender. If using fresh rather than frozen strawberries, add a few ice cubes, then process until smooth. Pour into a glass and decorate with extra slivered almonds, if desired.

Makes about 1¼ cups

nutty professor

1 cup lowfat milk
½ large banana
½ large mango
1 tablespoon peanut butter

Blend together all the ingredients with a couple of ice cubes for a silky, satisfying smoothie. To serve, decorate with slices of mango.

Makes about 1¼ cups

hippy shake

½ pineapple, about ½ lb
1 lemon
½ large avocado

Roughly chop the pineapple flesh and juice with the peeled lemon. Place the juice into a blender with the avocado and process until smooth. Serve with a slice of lemon, if desired.

Makes about ¾ cup

dried fruit salad smoothie

¾ cup dried fruit salad
1½ cups apple juice, more if necessary
¾ cup Greek yogurt

Roughly chop the fruit and place it in a large bowl. Pour over the apple juice, cover and let stand overnight. Put the dried fruit salad and apple juice in a food processor or blender. Add the yogurt and process until smooth, adding a little more apple juice if necessary. Pour into a glass and add a couple of ice cubes to chill.

Makes about 1⅔ cups

hippy shake

sleeping beauty

nutty professor

raspberry ripple

⅔ cup fresh raspberries
⅓ cup natural bio yogurt
⅓ cup soy milk

Whizz the raspberries, natural yogurt, and soy milk together in a blender until smooth. Swirl in a little yogurt to decorate.

Makes about 1¼ cups

energy store

1 cup canned peaches in grape juice
⅓ cup soy milk
1 tablespoon sunflower seeds

Put the peaches and their juice in a blender with the soy milk and sunflower seeds and process for about 20 seconds until smooth. Add a few ice cubes and blend again for about 10 seconds. Decorate with peach slices to serve.

Makes about 1¼ cups

cranberry, banana, and sesame smoothie

⅓ cup dried cranberries
½ lemon, juice only
1 large banana
1 tablespoon sesame seeds
2 tablespoons Greek yogurt
¾ cup whole or lowfat milk

Process the cranberries and lemon juice in a blender until the berries are finely chopped. Add the banana and sesame seeds, then puree, scraping the mixture down from the sides of the bowl if necessary. Add the yogurt and milk, processing until smooth and frothy. Decorate with dried cranberries, if desired.

Makes about 1¼ cups

apricot smoothie

1 cup canned apricots in natural juice, drained
⅔ cup apricot yogurt
⅔ cup ice-cold lowfat milk

Place the apricots, yogurt, and milk in a food processor or blender, and process until smooth. Add a couple of ice cubes, pour into a glass, and decorate with slices of apricot, if desired.

Makes about 1½ cups

raspberry ripple

energy store

*cranberry, banana,
and sesame smoothie*

Tropical Teasers

HULA KULA 28

SOUR GRAPES 28

BOLLYWOOD BLASTER 28

LOUNGE LIZARD 28

SILVER CLOUD 30

MANDARIN ORIENTAL 30

MELONBERRY 30

DRAMA QUEEN 30

MANGO LASSI 32

ATOMIC TONIC 32

FREE SPIRIT 32

CHOC BERRY 32

MOUNTAIN DREAMER 32

FRUIT FRAPPÉ 34

PUNCHBALL 34

KEY LIME PIE 34

BERRY SPRINGER 34

BLOCKBUSTER 34

MOODY BLUES 36

FRISKY SOUR 36

HI TENSION 36

LOVE POTION NO. 9 36

BANANA CALMER 38

ACHER SHAKER 38

COOL JUICE 38

TIME OUT 40

CUCUMBER AND MINT LASSI 40

WACKY WHIZZARD 40

MANGO, ORANGE, AND SOY MILKSHAKE 40

NEURO ZEN 40

hi tension (see page 36)

hula kula

½ pineapple, about ½ lb
⅓ cup coconut milk
⅓ cup soy milk

Place all the ingredients in a blender with some
ice cubes and blend until the mixture is smooth.
Decorate with pineapple leaves, if desired.

Makes about 1¼ cups

sour grapes

⅔ cup green or black grapes
⅓ cup cranberry juice
⅔ cup pitted cherries

Juice the grapes, then blend with the other
ingredients. Serve over ice and decorate with
fresh cherries, if desired.

Makes about 1 cup

bollywood blaster

¼ pineapple, about ¼ lb
½ small grapefruit
½ large banana

Juice the pineapple and grapefruit. Put the juice
into a blender with the banana and whizz.

Makes about 1 cup

lounge lizard

2½ kiwifruit
1 small cucumber
**1 tablespoon pomegranate seeds
(optional)**

Juice the kiwifruit and cucumber for a high
vitamin C drink. Serve with a slice of lime, to
decorate. If you wish, stir in a tablespoon of
pomegranate seeds.

Makes about ⅔ cup

lounge lizard

hula kula

sour grapes

silver cloud

½ **lemon**
⅓ **cup soy milk**
⅓ **cup ground almonds**
6 **canned litchis (drained)**

Juice the lemon and put it into a blender with the other ingredients and an ice cube. Blend until smooth and frothy. Serve decorated with lemon peel, if desired.

Makes about ¾ cup

mandarin oriental

I **large apple**
½ **cup canned mandarin segments (drained weight)**
5 **canned litchis (drained)**

Juice the apple, then blend with the mandarins and litchis. Add an ice cube and blend until smooth. Serve with ice cubes and mandarin segments, if desired.

Makes about I cup

melonberry

⅛ **watermelon, about 5 oz flesh**
I **cup raspberries**

Juice both fruits and serve over ice. Alternatively, whizz in a blender with ice to make a fruity slush. Serve decorated with mint, if desired.

Makes about ¾ cup

drama queen

¼ **watermelon, about ½–¾ lb flesh**
I **pomegranate**
⅔ **cup raspberries**

Scoop out the flesh of the melon and the pomegranate seeds. Juice with the raspberries and serve over ice. Decorate with pomegranate seeds, if desired.

Makes about ¾ cup

drama queen

silver cloud

mandarin oriental

free spirit

I medium lettuce
I large pear
2 kiwifruit

Juice all the ingredients and serve over ice decorated with a slice of lemon, if desired.

Makes about I ¼ cups

mango lassi

½ large mango
⅓ cup natural bio yogurt
⅓ cup water

Blend the mango flesh with the other ingredients until smooth, then serve decorated with mint.

Makes about I ⅓ cups

choc berry

¼ cup chocolate and hazelnut spread
¼ cup frozen strawberries
⅓ cup store-bought custard
⅓ cup soy milk

Whizz all the ingredients together in a blender until smooth and serve immediately. Decorate with a strawberry, to serve.

Makes about I cup

atomic tonic

I orange
½ lemon
½ large mango
⅔ cup canned mandarins (drained weight)

Juice the orange and lemon and then blend with the mango flesh and mandarins. Serve poured over ice and decorated with a basil leaf, if desired.

Makes about I ¼ cups

mountain dreamer

½ large pink grapefruit
6 canned litchis (drained)

Juice the grapefruit and place in a blender with the litchis. Blend until smooth. Pour into a glass and decorate with a slice of grapefruit, if desired.

Makes about ¾ cup

choc berry

mango lassi

mountain dreamer

fruit frappé

1 peach
1 pomegranate

Discard the peach pit and the skin of the pomegranate. Juice both ingredients and then blend with 2 or 3 ice cubes.

Makes about ¼ cup

punchball

2 celery sticks
⅔ cup green grapes
½ small avocado

Juice the celery and grapes. Put the juice into a blender with the avocado and serve with a couple of ice cubes and a celery leaf, if desired.

Makes about ¼ cup

key lime pie

1 kiwifruit
½ lime
⅓ cup soy milk

Juice the kiwifruit and the lime. Transfer to a blender and whizz with an ice cube and the soy milk.

Makes about ¼ cup

berry springer

⅔ cup frozen mixed berries
6 canned litchis (drained)
⅓ cup coconut milk
⅓ cup soy milk

Put all the ingredients in a blender with a couple of ice cubes and blend until smooth.

Makes about ¼ cup

blockbuster

2 tablespoons each of diced papaya, pineapple, carrot, sweet potato, apple, melon, grapefruit, and celery

Juice all the ingredients together and serve in a tall glass over ice. Decorate with slices of apple.

Makes about 1 cup

berry springer

blockbuster

punchball

moody blues

¾ lb blackberries
I small pineapple, about ¾ lb

Juice the blackberries first, then the pineapple. Blend the juices together with a couple of ice cubes and serve in a tall glass, decorated with a pineapple sliver, if desired.

Makes about ¼ cup

frisky sour

½ papaya
½ grapefruit
I cup raspberries
½ lime

Juice the flesh of the papaya with the grapefruit (pith left on) and the raspberries. Squeeze in the lime juice and mix together. Serve with a few ice cubes and, if desired, decorate with lime slices.

Makes about ¼ cup

hi tension

¼ pineapple, about 5 oz
3 celery sticks
½ lemon

Juice all the ingredients, then serve over ice in a tall glass. Decorate with sprigs of mint, if desired.

Makes about ¼ cup

love potion no. 9

½ lime
I small apple
I passion fruit
¼ papaya

Juice the lime, apple, and passion fruit pulp. Put the juice into a food processor or blender with the papaya flesh and blend until smooth.

Makes about ¼ cup

hi tension

moody blues

frisky sour

banana calmer

1 small banana
2 large oranges, juice only
2 tablespoons sunflower seeds

Put the banana, orange juice, and sunflower seeds into a blender with a few ice cubes and process until smooth. Serve in a large tumbler and decorate with some strawberry halves, if desired.

Makes about 1¼ cups

acher shaker

⅔ cup strawberries
½ pineapple, about ½ lb
1 banana

Juice the strawberries and pineapple. Pour the juice into a blender. Add the banana and a couple of ice cubes and process. Serve decorated with pineapple slices, if desired.

Makes about 1¼ cups

cool juice

⅔ cup strawberries
¼ watermelon, about ½–¾ lb flesh
½ small cucumber

Juice the strawberries, melon flesh, and cucumber. Serve over ice in a tall glass, decorated with cucumber slices, if desired.

Makes about ¾ cup

acher shaker

banana calmer

cool juice

time out

¼ cantaloupe melon
⅔ cup fresh or frozen blackberries
2 kiwifruit

Juice the melon flesh, blackberries, and kiwifruit; then put the juices in a blender and process with a couple of ice cubes. Pour into a glass and serve decorated with a few blackberries, if desired.

Makes about 1 cup

cucumber and mint lassi

1 medium cucumber
1 cup natural bio yogurt
handful of chopped mint
¼ teaspoon salt (optional)

Remove and discard the cucumber seeds. Place the flesh in a blender with the yogurt, mint, and salt, if using, and process until smooth. Pour into a glass, add a couple of ice cubes, and decorate with mint, if desired.

Makes about 1¼ cups

wacky whizzard

½ large mango
2 small apples
1 small cucumber

Juice the ingredients, then blend with a couple of ice cubes to make a fruity slush.

Makes about ¾ cup

mango, orange, and soy milkshake

1 small mango
1 orange, juice only
⅔ cup soy milk
1–2 teaspoons honey

Scoop the mango flesh into a blender with the orange juice, soy milk, and 1 teaspoon of honey. Process until smooth, scraping the sides if necessary. Taste for sweetness, and add more honey, if desired.

Makes about 1¼ cups

neuro zen

1½ cups white grapes
1 medium lettuce
1 inch cube fresh ginger root, roughly chopped

Juice all the ingredients. Serve over ice, or pour into a blender and process with ice cubes for a zingy icy slush. Decorate with white or red grapes, if desired.

Makes about ¾ cup

time out

wacky whizzard

neuro zen

Veggie Juices

cool down (see page 44)

green light

¼ lb broccoli
1 small apple
1 small cucumber

Juice the broccoli with the apple and cucumber and serve in a tall glass. Decorate with cucumber slivers, if desired.

Makes about ¼ cup

cool down

2 small carrots
2 beets
½ yam or 1 small sweet potato
1 small Florence fennel bulb

Juice all the ingredients. Mix the energy-boosting juices together and serve in a glass with ice cubes. Decorate with fennel fronds, if desired.

Makes about ¼ cup

six pack

¼ lb asparagus stalks
10 dandelion leaves
¼ Galia or honeydew melon
1 medium cucumber
1 large pear

Trim the woody bits off the asparagus stalks. Roll the dandelion leaves into a ball and juice them (if you have picked wild leaves, wash them first) with the asparagus. Juice the melon flesh, cucumber, and pear. Whizz all the juices in a blender and serve in a tall glass with ice cubes.

Makes about ¼ cup

root 66

2 small carrots
1 parsnip
3 celery sticks
1 small sweet potato
a handful of parsley
1 garlic clove

Juice all the ingredients together, then whizz in a blender with 2 ice cubes. Serve in a short glass decorated with a wedge of lemon and a parsley sprig, if desired.

Makes about ¼ cup

green light

six pack

cool down

root 66

loosen up 1

1½ inch cube fresh horseradish
½ lemon, juice only

Pulverize the horseradish by juicing a small amount and mixing the juice and the pulp to make about 1½ teaspoons of puree. Put it into a shot glass and stir in the lemon juice.

Makes about 3 tablespoons

hot stuff

2 medium tomatoes, about ¾ lb
2 celery sticks
1 inch cube fresh ginger root, roughly
   chopped
1 garlic clove
1 inch cube fresh horseradish
2 small carrots

Juice all the ingredients, then blend with 2 ice cubes and serve in a tumbler. Decorate with celery slivers, if desired.

Makes about ⅔ cup

loosen up 2

2 small carrots
¾ cup radishes, with tops and leaves
1 inch cube fresh ginger root, roughly
   chopped (optional)

Juice the carrots, radishes, and ginger, if using. Add some ice cubes. Drink one hour after Loosen Up 1.

Makes about ¾ cup

earth mother

1 carrot
1 small lettuce
1 small parsnip
¼ cantaloupe melon

Juice the carrot, lettuce, and parsnip with the flesh of the melon. Mix thoroughly and serve in a tall glass with ice and wedges of melon, if desired.

Makes about 1 cup

These two juices are great if you have a cold and should be taken in tandem.

hot stuff

loosen up 2

earth mother

loosen up 1

head banger

I medium lettuce
I small Florence fennel bulb
½ lemon

Juice the lettuce, fennel, and lemon. Mix well and serve poured over ice. Decorate with lemon rind slivers and lettuce leaves, if desired.

Makes about ⅔ cup

heart beet

2 large beets
I cup watercress
I small red onion
3 small carrots
I garlic clove

Juice all the ingredients and serve mixed together in a tall glass. Garnish with beet leaves and watercress, if desired.

Makes about ¼ cup

famous 5

¼ lb Brussels sprouts
I carrot
¼ lb Jerusalem artichokes
¼ lb green beans
I small lettuce
½ lemon

Juice all the vegetables together with the lemon. Serve garnished with slivers of green bean and carrot, if desired.

Makes about ¼ cup

head banger

heart beet

famous 5

iron maiden

½ lb spinach
⅓ cup parsley
3 small carrots
I teaspoon spirulina

Juice the spinach, parsley, and carrots, and stir in the spirulina. Serve in a tumbler, decorated with carrot slivers if desired.

Makes about ¼ cup

sleep tight

¼ pineapple, about ¼ lb
¾ cup grapes
½ small lettuce
I celery stick

Juice all the ingredients and serve in a tall glass over ice. Decorate with lettuce leaves, if desired.

Makes about ¼ cup

well healed

3 small carrots
½ lb green cabbage

Juice the vegetables and serve in a tall glass, over ice. Decorate with a few shreds of cabbage.

Makes about ¼ cup

sticks and stones

¼ lb turnips, including the tops
I carrot
¼ lb broccoli
handful of dandelion leaves
2 small apples

Juice all the ingredients, then whizz in a blender with a couple of ice cubes. Serve in a tall glass decorated with dandelion leaves, if desired.

Makes about ¼ cup

iron maiden

sleep tight

hot potato

I small potato, cooked
¼ lb radishes
I small carrot
½ medium cucumber

Juice the ingredients together and then whizz in a blender with 2 ice cubes. Serve in a tall glass garnished with radish slices, if desired.

Makes about ¼ cup

twister

½ pink grapefruit
I large carrot
¼ lb spinach

Peel the grapefruit, keeping as much of the pith as possible. Juice all the ingredients and serve in a tumbler, decorated with grapefruit slices, if desired.

Makes about ¼ cup

herbi-four

I red bell pepper, seeded
I large tomato
¼ lb white cabbage
I tablespoon chopped parsley

Juice the bell pepper, tomato, and cabbage. Pour into a tall glass. Stir in the parsley and serve with ice cubes and a lime wedge, if desired.

Makes about ¼ cup

hard as nails

I small parsnip
I green bell pepper, seeded
¾ cup watercress
¾ medium cucumber

Juice the ingredients together and serve over ice with a sprinkling of mint, if desired.

Makes about ¼ cup

twister

herbi-four

hot potato

hard as nails

vision impeccable

2 small carrots
¼ lb endive
2 celery sticks

Juice the carrot, endive and celery. Whizz in a food processor or blender with a couple of ice cubes and serve over ice garnished with lemon slices and some chopped parsley, if desired.

Makes about ¼ cup

what's up broc?

½ lb broccoli
2 small carrots
1 small beet

Juice all the ingredients together and then serve in a tall glass. Add crushed ice and garnish with a cilantro sprig, if desired.

Makes about ¼ cup

chili queen

2 carrots
½ small seeded chili or a sprinkling of chili powder
½ pineapple, about ½ lb
½ lime, juice only
1 tablespoon chopped cilantro leaves

Juice the carrots, chili, and pineapple. Pour into a tall glass over ice cubes. Squeeze in the lime juice and stir in the chopped cilantro leaves to serve.

Makes about ¼ cup

hangover express

¼ lb broccoli
2 apples
¼ lb spinach

Juice the broccoli, apples, and spinach, alternating the spinach leaves with the broccoli and apple to prevent the machine from clogging up with the leaves. Blend the juice with a couple of ice cubes, and serve with ice and a slice of lemon, if desired.

Makes about ¼ cup

vision impeccable

chili queen

hangover express

what's up broc?

squeaky green

2 carrots
2 celery sticks
¼ lb spinach
I small lettuce
⅓ cup parsley

Juice the ingredients and whizz in a blender with a couple of ice cubes. Decorate with parsley sprigs, if desired.

Makes about ¾ cup

tranquillizer

I romaine lettuce
2 apples

Juice the lettuce and apples. Place ice cubes in a tall glass and pour the juice over them. Serve immediately, decorated with apple slices, if desired.

Makes about ¾ cup

veg out

¼ lb cauliflower
2 small carrots
I large tomato

Juice the cauliflower, carrots, and tomato. Stir to mix, then serve poured over ice and garnished with carrot tops, if desired.

Makes about ¾ cup

stress buster

⅓ lb spinach
⅓ lb broccoli
2 tomatoes

Juice the spinach, broccoli, and tomatoes, then mix together. Serve in a tumbler over ice, decorated with sliced tomatoes, if desired.

Makes about ¾ cup

stress buster

squeaky green

veg out

upbeet

¼ lb celeriac, peeled
I medium beet
I carrot
½ cup radicchio
I apple

Juice all the ingredients, then process the juice in a blender with a couple of ice cubes. Decorate with slivers of radicchio, if desired.

Makes about ¼ cup

gargle blaster

¼ lb celeriac
¼ lb Jerusalem artichokes
2 celery sticks
small bunch of mint

Juice the vegetables and the mint, alternating the mint leaves with the other ingredients to prevent the juicer getting clogged up. Process the juice in a blender with ice cubes and serve decorated with celery sticks, if desired.

Makes about ¼ cup

spring clean

2 small pears
¼ lb cabbage
I celery stick
8 sprigs watercress

Juice all the ingredients together. Serve over ice decorated with celery sticks, if desired.

Makes about ¾ cup

go with the flow

3 celery sticks
8 sprigs rocket
8 sprigs watercress
I apple
½ small avocado

Juice the celery, rocket, watercress, and apple. Put the juice in a blender with the avocado and a couple of ice cubes and process until smooth. Decorate with a slice of lime, if desired.

Makes about ¾ cup

spring clean

upbeet

go with the flow

Citrus Juices

the rehydrator (see page 70)

navel cadet

I lime
2 small oranges
½ large mango

Juice the lime and oranges, and whizz in a food processor or blender together with the mango flesh and an ice cube. Decorate with lime slices, if desired.

Makes about I cup

bitter sweet

½ large grapefruit
I small parsnip
I small sweet potato

Juice all the ingredients and blend the juice with an ice cube. Serve over ice and, if desired, decorate with a sliver of parsnip.

Makes about ¼ cup

karma fruitra

½ grapefruit
2 fresh figs
½ small orange
½ lemon

Juice all the fruit, then blend with an ice cube to chill. Decorate with slices of fig, if desired.

Makes about ¼ cup

chill pill

I small Florence fennel bulb
I lemon
⅓ cup chilled chamomile tea

Juice the fennel and lemon, then mix with the chamomile tea. Serve over ice with some lemon slices, if desired.

Makes about ¼ cup

bitter sweet

karma fruitra

navel cadet

ginger zinger

1 carrot
½ Galia or honeydew melon
1 lime
1 inch cube fresh ginger root, roughly
chopped

Juice the carrot, melon flesh, lime, and ginger. Serve in a glass over ice. Decorate with lime wedges and seeds from a cardamom pod, if desired.

Makes about ¾ cup

sergeant pepper

½ red bell pepper, seeded
½ yellow bell pepper, seeded
½ orange bell pepper, seeded
1 orange
1 tablespoon mint leaves

Juice the peppers and orange, and serve in a tumbler with ice cubes. Stir in the mint and decorate with more mint leaves, if desired.

Makes about ¾ cup

carrot and pink grapefruit

1 pink grapefruit
2 carrots
2 apples
1½ cups water

Juice the carrots, apples, and grapefruit, then add the water. Pour the juice into a glass and add a couple of ice cubes. Decorate with apple slices, if desired.

Makes about 3 cups

all systems go

¼ watermelon, about ½–¾ lb flesh
2 oranges

Juice the fruit, pour it into a glass, and add a couple of ice cubes to chill. Decorate with slices of orange, if desired.

Makes about 1¼ cups

ginger zinger

sergeant pepper

all systems go

live wire

2 oranges
1 red apple
1 pear
1 teaspoon clear honey (optional)

Juice the fruit and pour it into a glass. Stir in the honey, if using, and add a couple of ice cubes. Decorate with orange slices, if desired.

Makes about 1⅓ cups

pear and pineapple

2 pears
½ lime
½ pineapple, about ½ lb

Juice all the fruit. Then pour into a glass. Add some ice cubes and decorate with wedges of pineapple, if desired.

Makes about 1¼ cups

orange and raspberry

2 large oranges
1¼ cups raspberries
1 cup water

Juice the fruit, then add the water to dilute. Pour into 2 glasses and add a couple of ice cubes to each.

Makes about 2 cups

strawberry, redcurrant, and orange

⅔ cup strawberries, hulled
⅓ cup redcurrants, hulled
½ orange
½ cup water
½ teaspoon clear honey (optional)

Juice the fruit, then add the water. Pour into a glass. Stir in the honey, if using, and add some ice cubes to create a refreshing fatigue-defying drink. Decorate with redcurrants, if desired.

Makes about 1 cup

live wire

strawberry, redcurrant, and orange

orange and apricot

6 apricots
I large orange
I¼ cups water

Juice the fruit, then add the water. Pour into a glass and add ice cubes to chill, if desired.

Makes about 2½ cups

sweet chariot

¼ pineapple, about ¼ lb
⅔ cup grapes
I small orange
I small apple
½ large mango
½ large banana

Juice the pineapple, grapes, orange, and apple. Whizz in a blender with the mango, banana, and a couple of ice cubes for a super sweet smoothie. Serve decorated with orange wedges and strips of mint, if desired.

Makes about 1½ cups

orange, cranberry, and mango

I¼ cups cranberries
I mango
I orange
⅓ cup water
I teaspoon clear honey

Juice the fruit, pour into a glass, and stir in the water and honey. Add a couple of ice cubes to chill and decorate with cranberries, if desired.

Makes about 1½ cups

citron xpresse

I lemon
⅔ cup green grapes

Juice both ingredients then make up to ¾ cup with cold water. Serve over ice. If you like, add hot water instead to make a hot toddy.

Makes about ¾ cup

karma kooler

2 grapefruit
I large cucumber
I lemon
sparkling mineral water

Juice the grapefruit, cucumber, and lemon. Pour into a jug over ice, and top up with sparkling mineral water to make up to about 1½ cups. Decorate with mint and slices of cucumber and lemon, if desired.

Makes about 1½ cups

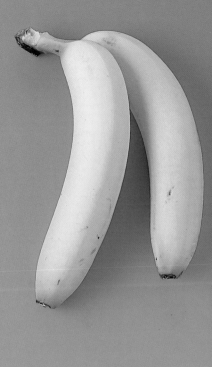

citron xpresse

karma kooler

sweet chariot

mind bath

I romaine lettuce
½ lemon
⅓ cup chilled chamomile tea

Juice the lettuce and lemon, then mix with the chilled chamomile tea. Serve in a tall glass over ice with slices of lemon, if desired.

Makes about ¼ cup

pulpitation

I large orange
½ grapefruit
I lime

Juice the fruit (and a little of the pith), then serve poured over ice. If you want a longer drink, dilute with an equal amount of sparkling mineral water. Decorate with curls of lime rind, if desired.

Makes about ¼ cup

the rehydrator

I orange
¼ small cucumber
⅓ cup cranberry juice

Juice the orange (with as much of its pith as possible) and cucumber. Mix this juice with the cranberry juice. Serve in a tall glass over ice, decorated with slices of cucumber, if desired.

Makes about ¼ cup

pulpitation

the rehydrator

mind bath

calm seas

2 oranges
I kiwifruit
I cup strawberries

Juice the oranges (with as much of their pith as possible) with the kiwifruit (skin left on) and the strawberries. Decorate with strawberry slices.

Makes about ¾ cup

c double

2 large oranges
2 kiwifruit

Juice the oranges (with as much of their pith as possible) with the kiwifruit (skins left on). Serve over ice with some kiwifruit slices, if desired.

Makes about ¾ cup

vitamin vitality

I carrot
2 oranges

Juice the carrot with the oranges and serve decorated with a slice of orange.

Makes about ¾ cup

mother nature

½ grapefruit
2 celery sticks
I small Florence fennel bulb

Juice the grapefruit, celery, and fennel. Serve in a tall glass over ice with a slice of pink grapefruit, if desired.

Makes about ¾ cup

butterfly kiss

¼ Galia or honeydew melon
I lemon
I inch cube fresh ginger root, roughly chopped

Juice the melon flesh, the lemon, and the ginger, and serve over ice.

Makes about ¾ cup

double

vitamin vitality

mother nature

Breakfast in a Glass

morning dew (see page 88)

plum punch

1 peach
2 plums
1 kiwifruit

Juice all the ingredients and serve over ice cubes. Decorate with plum slices, if desired.

Makes about ¼ cup

sour power

1 pomegranate
1 carrot
⅔ cup grapes

Scoop out the pomegranate pulp and seeds, then juice with the carrot and grapes. Serve with crushed ice and decorate with pomegranate seeds, if desired.

Makes about ¼ cup

green dream

2 large apples
1 celery stick
½ kiwifruit
½ lemon
1 small avocado

Juice the apple, celery, kiwifruit, and lemon. Transfer to a blender and whizz with the avocado for 20 seconds to make a refreshing smoothie. Decorate with kiwi slices, if desired.

Makes about ¼ cup

sour power

plum punch

mellow yellow

I small apple
2 celery sticks
I ½ cups alfalfa sprouts

Juice all the ingredients and serve in a tall glass. Decorate with a sprinkle of alfalfa sprouts, if desired.

Makes about I cup

kiwi quencher

I kiwifruit
⅔ cup grapes
2 celery sticks
½ lemon

Juice all the ingredients together and serve poured over ice. If desired, decorate with celery slices.

Makes about ⅔ cup

papaya flyer

½ large pear
I carrot
¼ papaya

Juice the pear and carrot and put in a blender with the papaya and an ice cube and blend until smooth. Decorate with thin slices of pear, if desired.

Makes about ¼ cup

red eye

2 large tomatoes, about ½ lb
I small Florence fennel bulb
I small scallion
I tablespoon coriander
black pepper
Tabasco sauce

Juice the tomatoes, fennel, scallion, and coriander together before serving with a sprinkling of black pepper and a splash of Tabasco sauce.

Makes about ¼ cup

papaya flyer

mellow yellow

kiwi quencher

purple passion

½ lb blueberries
½ grapefruit
2 large apples
I inch cube fresh ginger root, roughly
chopped

Juice all the ingredients together and serve in a tall glass with ice cubes. Decorate with thin slices of ginger, if desired.

Makes about ¼ cup

easy does it

2 small pears
I bunch watercress
½ lemon

Juice all the ingredients and serve in a small glass over ice. Add a twist of lemon, if desired.

Makes about 3 tablespoons

peach fizz

2 peaches
I inch cube fresh ginger root, roughly
chopped
sparkling mineral water

Juice the peach and ginger and serve in a tall glass over ice. Add a splash of sparkling water, a couple of mint leaves and slices of peach, if desired.

Makes about ¼ cup

strawberry sunrise

½ lb strawberries
2 small oranges

Juice the strawberries and oranges. Serve straight over ice, or blend with a couple of ice cubes for a thicker drink. Decorate with whole strawberries, if desired.

Makes about ¼ cup

way to go

2 small pears
¼ cup pitted prunes
¼ lb spinach

Juice all the ingredients and serve in a glass over ice cubes. Decorate with pear slices, if desired.

Makes about ¼ cup

hazy days

I large pear
⅓ cup cranberry juice

Juice the pear and mix with the cranberry juice. Serve in a tall glass over ice and decorate with cranberries, if desired.

Makes about ¼ cup

hazy days

way to go

peach fizz

purple passion

c breeze

½ grapefruit
½ kiwifruit
¼ pineapple, about 6 oz
½ cup frozen raspberries
⅓ cup frozen cranberries

Juice the grapefruit, kiwifruit, and pineapple, then whizz in a blender with the frozen berries to make a thick smoothie. Decorate with raspberries, if desired, and serve with drinking straws.

Makes about ¾ cup

morning after

¼ papaya
2 oranges
½ small cucumber

Juice the papaya flesh and orange (with as much pith as possible) with the cucumber and serve in a tall glass over ice. Decorate with slices of cucumber and papaya, if desired.

Makes about ¾ cup

ginger spice

3 carrots
½ small Florence fennel bulb
1 large celery stick
1 inch cube fresh ginger root, roughly chopped
1 tablespoon spirulina (optional)

Juice the ingredients and serve over ice. If desired, decorate with strips of fennel and fennel fronds. Add 1 tablespoon of spirulina if you want to suppress your appetite.

Makes about ¾ cup

quantum leap

2 large apples
1 inch cube fresh ginger root, roughly chopped

Juice the apple and ginger and serve in a glass over ice. Decorate with some chopped mint, if desired. This drink can be diluted with sparkling mineral water to taste.

Makes about ½ cup

morning after   *c breeze*

ginger spice

green peace

¼ lb broccoli
¼ lb kale
⅓ cup parsley
2 apples
I celery stick

Juice all the ingredients and serve in a glass over ice. Decorate with sprigs of curly kale, if desired.

Makes about ¾ cup

full tank

¼ pineapple, about ¼ lb
I small apple
I½ cups alfalfa sprouts
⅓ cup soy milk

Juice the pineapple, apple, and alfalfa sprouts together. Put the juice into a blender with the soy milk and an ice cube and blend. Serve in a tall glass.

Makes about I¼ cups

morning glory

½ cantaloupe melon (or any melon)

Juice the melon flesh and seeds for an enlivening breakfast drink, then serve over ice. Drink immediately.

Makes about I¼ cups

apple and blackberry

3 apples
I cup blackberries
I¼ cups water

Juice the fruit, then stir in the water. Pour into a glass and add a couple of ice cubes to chill.

Makes about 2½ cups

full tank   *green peace*

morning glory

eye opener

2 carrots
I small Florence fennel bulb

Juice the carrots and fennel. Serve the juice in a tall glass over ice and decorated with fennel, if desired.

Makes about ¼ cup

pink grapefruit and pineapple

I pink grapefruit
½ pineapple, about ½ lb
1¼ cups water

Juice the grapefruit and pineapple, then stir in the water. Pour into 2 glasses and add a couple of ice cubes to each glass.

Makes about 2½ cups

strawberry and kiwifruit

¾ cup strawberries, hulled
2 kiwifruit, peeled

Juice the strawberries and kiwifruit flesh together. Pour into a glass and add ice cubes, if desired.

Makes about 1¼ cups

water baby

¼ watermelon, about ½–¾ lb flesh
¼ lb raspberries

Juice the watermelon flesh and raspberries. Pour into a large glass and add a couple of ice cubes.

Makes about 1½ cups

water baby

eye opener

tummy tickler

3 small apples
1¼ cups blackcurrants

Juice the fruit and serve over ice for a great blackcurrant cordial substitute. Decorate with extra blackcurrants, if desired.

Makes about ¾ cup

morning dew

3 celery sticks
¼ Galia or honeydew melon

Juice both ingredients to make a sweetly refreshing drink and serve with a twist of lemon.

Makes about ¾ cup

berry nice

2 bananas
1¼ cups raspberries
¾ cup blueberries
1 small glass cranberry juice
2 tablespoons natural bio yogurt (optional)

Roughly chop the bananas and put into a blender. Add the berries and pour in the cranberry juice. Blend until smooth. Add the yogurt for a thicker creamier drink.

Makes about 1¼ cups

bumpy ride

2 small apples
1 small beet
2 celery sticks

Juice all the ingredients and serve over ice in a tumbler. Decorate with apple slices, if desired.

Makes about ⅔ cup

morning dew

bumpy ride

Here's to Good Health

clear ahead (see page 98)

grapple juice

1 apple
⅔ cup green grapes

Juice both ingredients for a simple, healthy drink, then serve over ice. Decorate with apple slices, if desired.

Makes about ¼ cup

carrot and kiwifruit

2 carrots
1 kiwifruit

Juice the carrots and kiwifruit. Pour into a glass and add a couple of ice cubes. Decorate with slices of kiwifruit, if desired.

Makes about 1 cup

red devil

½ large tomato, about ¼ lb
¼ Galia or honeydew melon
1 carrot

Juice the tomato, melon flesh, and carrot. Serve over ice with fresh chilies, if desired.

Makes about 1 cup

purple heart

2 small beets
¼ melon (any type)
2 small plums

Juice all the ingredients and then transfer to a blender. Add an ice cube and whizz for a thicker drink. Serve in a tall glass.

Makes about 1¼ cups

grapple juice

purple heart

red devil

beetnik

2 small beets
⅓ cup grapes
1 orange

Juice all ingredients and serve in a tumbler with ice to chill. Decorate with an orange slice, if desired.

Makes about ¾ cup

city slicker

1 parsnip
1 small Florence fennel bulb
1 medium cucumber

Juice all the ingredients and serve over ice with mint, if desired.

Makes about ¾ cup

grape expectation

½ small pear
⅓ cup red grapes
¼ cup blackberries

Juice the fruit together and serve over ice.

Makes about ¾ cup

mr green

½ lb broccoli
1½ cups green grapes

Juice both ingredients and serve over ice, decorated with mint.

Makes about ¾ cup

mystic mango

⅔ cup green grapes
1 small Florence fennel bulb
½ large mango

Juice the grapes and fennel, then put into a blender with the mango and a couple of ice cubes and blend to make a replenishing icy smoothie. Serve with fennel fronds, if desired.

Makes about 1¼ cups

mystic mango

beetnik

city slicker

fireball

¾ cup raspberries
I small Florence fennel bulb
I small pear
I inch cube fresh ginger root, roughly chopped

Juice all the ingredients together to make a sweet, spicy drink and serve.

Makes about ¼ cup

autumn leaf

I small peach
2 celery sticks
I small orange

Juice the peach, celery, and orange together. Serve poured over ice. Decorate with slices of peach, if desired.

Makes about ¼ cup

slow burn

I celery stick
¼ parsnip
⅓ cup pineapple
¾ cup lettuce
⅓ cup grapes

Juice all the ingredients together and serve in a short tumbler. Serve with slivers of pineapple, if desired.

Makes about ⅔ cup

orangatang

I small orange
I carrot
½ sweet potato
I inch cube fresh ginger root, roughly chopped

Juice the orange with the carrot, sweet potato, and ginger. Serve poured over ice. Decorate with a slice of orange, if desired.

Makes about ¼ cup

autumn leaf

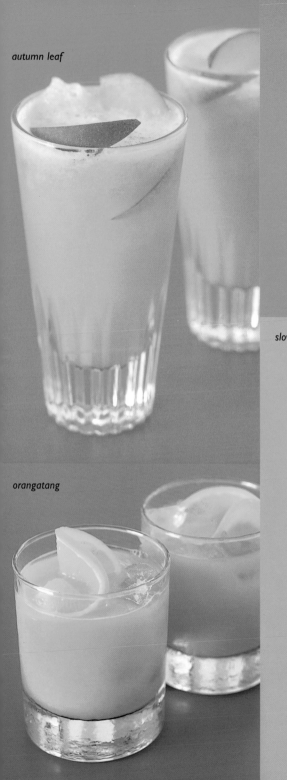

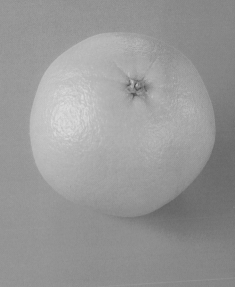

slow burn

orangatang

panic attack

2 apples
3 apricots
1 peach

Juice the apples, apricots, and peach. Pour into a blender with a few ice cubes and whizz for 10 seconds. Serve in a tall glass and decorate with peach slices, if desired.

Makes about ¼ cup

culture shock

2 large apples
1 cup frozen cranberries
⅓ cup live natural bio yogurt
1 tablespoon clear honey

Juice the apple and whizz in a blender with the other ingredients for a fresh-tasting smoothie. Serve in a tumbler over ice cubes.

Makes about ¼ cup

passion thriller

½ Galia or honeydew melon
½ medium cucumber
1 small avocado
⅓ cup dried apricots
1 tablespoon wheatgerm

Juice the melon and cucumber. Whizz in a blender with the avocado, apricots, wheatgerm, and a couple of ice cubes. Decorate with dried apricot slivers, if desired.

Makes about ¼ cup

clear ahead

2 large carrots
½ cup radishes
1 large apple

Juice the carrots, radishes, and apple. Pour the juice into a blender and process with a couple of ice cubes. Serve decorated with slices of apple, if desired.

Makes about ¼ cup

panic attack

passion thriller

clear ahead

culture shock

summer breeze

⅓ Galia melon
I small Florence fennel bulb

Juice both ingredients for a light fresh drink
and serve over ice. Serve with slivers of fennel,
if desired.

Makes about ¼ cup

pick-me-up

2 carrots
I tart-flavored apple
½ inch piece fresh ginger root, roughly
chopped

Juice the carrots, apple and ginger. Pour into a
glass and add a couple of ice cubes, and decorate
with apple, if desired.

Makes about I cup

carrot, orange, and apple

2 carrots
I orange
I tart-flavored apple

Juice all the fruit and pour into a glass, then add a
couple of ice cubes.

Makes about I cup

summer breeze

pick-me-up

celery and tomato

2 celery sticks
4 tomatoes
large handful of parsley
½ lemon, rind and juice

Feed the celery, tomatoes, and parsley into the juicer in alternate batches, along with the lemon juice and rind. Pour the juice into a glass and add a couple of ice cubes.

Makes about 1¼ cups

ultimate detox

4 carrots
2 green apples

Juice both the ingredients and serve in a tall glass over ice for a great cleansing drink. Decorate with slices of apple, if desired.

Makes about 1¼ cups

strawberry, peach, and apple

⅔ cup strawberries, hulled
2 peaches
1 red apple
1¼ cups water

Juice the strawberries, peaches, and apple. Add the water and mix well, then pour the juice into a glass and add ice cubes, if desired.

Makes about 2½ cups

scarlet woman

2 small beets
⅔ cup strawberries
1 small apple

Juice all the ingredients and serve decorated with a twist of apple peel, if desired.

Makes about 1¼ cups

ultimate detox

scarlet woman

flush-a-bye-baby

2 cups cranberries
¼ watermelon or ½ Galia melon
½ lb cucumber

Juice all the ingredients, including the seeds of the melon and the skin of the cucumber. Serve in a tumbler and decorate with melon sticks, if desired.

Makes about ¾ cup

healing hand

2 pears
3 kiwifruit, peeled
½ lime

Use ripe pears, if possible. Juice them with the kiwifruit flesh. Pour into a glass. Add a couple of ice cubes and decorate with slices of kiwifruit, if desired.

Makes about 1¼ cups

red-hot remedy

4 large tomatoes
1 apple
1 celery stick
4 basil leaves, finely chopped
1½ tablespoons lime juice

Juice the tomatoes, apple, and celery. Pour into a glass over ice and stir in the basil and lime juice.

Makes about ¾ cup

apple and plum

5 eating plums
3 red apples

Choose ripe plums if possible. Juice them with the apple and serve in a glass poured over a couple of ice cubes.

Makes about 1¼ cups

healing hand

flush-a-bye-baby

Hi-Energy Boosters

juicy lucy (see page 120)

back on track

1 small sweet potato
2 small oranges
1 large carrot

Juice the sweet potato, oranges, and carrots. To make a smoother, creamier drink, transfer the juice to a blender and process with a couple of ice cubes. Decorate with mint sprigs, if desired.

Makes about ¾ cup

evergreen

1 celery stick
2 Florence fennel stalks
1 romaine lettuce
½ pineapple, about ½ lb
1 teaspoon chopped tarragon

Juice all the ingredients and whizz in a blender with 2 ice cubes. Serve in a tall glass, decorated with tarragon sprigs, if desired.

Makes about ¾ cup

power pack

3 small carrots
2 beets, about ¼ lb
1 orange
¼ lb strawberries

Juice the carrots, beets, and orange together. Put the juice into a blender with a couple of ice cubes and the strawberries. Whizz for 20 seconds and serve in a tall glass. Decorate with strips of orange rind, if desired.

Makes about ¾ cup

grape and plum

1 cup seedless red grapes
5 plums

Juice the grapes and plums together, and pour into a glass. Add a couple of ice cubes and decorate with slices of plum, if desired.

Makes about ¾ cup

back on track

evergreen

power pack

magnificent 7

1 carrot
½ green bell pepper, seeded
1 cup spinach leaves
1 small onion
1 celery stick
⅓ medium cucumber
½ small tomato
sea salt and pepper

Juice the ingredients and season with sea salt and pepper for the ultimate healthy pick-me-up. If desired, decorate with tomato quarters.

Makes about ¾ cup

liven up

½ Galia melon
½ pineapple, about ½ lb
1 green apple

Juice the flesh of the melon and pineapple with the apple. Pour into a glass and add a couple of ice cubes. Decorate with apple slices, if desired.

Makes about 1¼ cups

high kick

½ lb strawberries
1 kiwifruit
½ large banana
1 tablespoon spirulina powder
1 tablespoon linseeds

Juice the strawberries and kiwifruit and whizz in a blender with the banana, spirulina, linseeds and a couple of ice cubes. Decorate with redcurrants and linseeds, if desired.

Makes about ¾ cup

red velvet

½ large red bell pepper, seeded
¼ lb strawberries
½ small tomato
½ large mango
⅛ watermelon, about ¼ lb flesh

Juice all the ingredients, then whizz in a blender with 3 ice cubes and serve in a tall glass. Decorate with mango slices, if desired.

Makes about ¾ cup

liven up

red velvet

high kick

watercress and pear

3 pears
1 cup watercress

Choose ripe pears if possible. Feed the pear chunks and watercress into the juicer in alternate batches. Pour into a glass and add ice cubes. Decorate with watercress leaves, if desired.

Makes about 1 cup

energy bubble

3 apples, preferably red
1 mango
2 passion fruit

Juice the apples and mango with the passion fruit flesh (discard the seeds). Pour the juice into a glass and add a couple of ice cubes. Decorate with apple slices, if desired.

Makes about 1¼ cups

beet, apple, and carrot

2 small beets
1 carrot
2 apples
1¼ cups water

Juice the beetroot, carrot and apples. Add the water, mix well then pour into a glass. Add a couple of ice cubes to chill.

Makes about 2½ cups

celery, tomato, and red bell pepper

3 tomatoes, about 1 lb
4 celery sticks
½ red bell pepper, seeded
½ red chili, seeded (optional)
1 garlic clove, crushed (optional)

Choose ripe tomatoes if possible. Juice them with the celery and red bell pepper. Pour into a glass. Stir in the chili and crushed garlic, if using, and add a couple of ice cubes, if desired.

Makes about 1¼ cups

watercress and pear

energy bubble

celery, tomato, and red
bell pepper

sky high

½ lime, unpeeled
2 pears
½ pineapple, about ½ lb

Scrub the lime and juice it with the pears and pineapple flesh. Pour into a glass. Add a couple of ice cubes and decorate with pinapple, if desired.

Makes about 1¼ cups

energy burst

¼ lb spinach
2 large apples
½ yellow bell pepper, seeded
a pinch of cinnamon

Juice all the ingredients for a fatigue-fighting drink and serve in a tall glass. If desired, add cinnamon sticks for decoration.

Makes about ¼ cup

red wire

⅔ cup red grapes
2 small beets
2 small plums

Juice the grapes, beets, and plums together and serve in a tumbler over ice. Decorate with plum slices, if desired.

Makes about ¼ cup

energy burst

red wire

sky high

melon, kiwifruit, and grape

½ honeydew melon
2 kiwifruit, peeled
¾ cup seedless green grapes

Juice the flesh of the melon and kiwifruit with the grapes. Pour into a glass and add ice cubes. Serve with slices of kiwifruit, if desired.

Makes about 1¼ cups

whizzical

1 banana
¾ cup soy milk
⅓ cup ground almonds

Put all the ingredients in a blender with 2 ice cubes and blend until smooth. Serve sprinkled with cinnamon flakes, if desired.

Makes about 1¼ cups

marathon man

½ Galia melon
1¼ cups seedless green grapes
1¼ cups water

Juice the melon flesh with the grapes. Mix in the water and pour into 2 glasses. Add a couple of ice cubes and decorate with grapes, if desired.

Makes about 2½ cups

marathon man

whizzical

melon, kiwifruit, and grape

deep breath

1 large tomato
½ red bell pepper, seeded
¼ papaya

Juice the tomato, red bell pepper, and papaya flesh. Pour the juice into a food processor or blender. Add a couple of ice cubes and process. Serve decorated with slivers of red bell pepper, if desired.

Makes about ¾ cup

raw energy

1 small tomato
½ lb cabbage
large handful of parsley
1 celery stick (optional)

Juice the tomato, cabbage and parsley together and serve in a tumbler. Add sliced tomatoes or a stick of celery, to garnish.

Makes about ¾ cup

invigorate

2 oranges
½ lemon
½ inch cube fresh ginger root, roughly chopped
2 small beets
¼ lb spinach
2 celery sticks
1 carrot

Juice all the ingredients together. Serve decorated with orange rind curls, if desired.

Makes about 2½ cups

red rocket

2 small carrots
2 large apples
¼ lb red cabbage

Juice all the ingredients together. Serve over ice in a tall glass and decorate with slivers of red cabbage, if desired.

Makes about ¾ cup

deep breath

invigorate

red rocket

raw energy

celery, apple, and alfalfa

3 celery sticks
2 tart-flavored apples
½ cup alfalfa sprouts

Feed all the ingredients into a juicer in alternate batches. Pour into a glass. Add a couple of ice cubes and drink immediately.

Makes about 1 cup

battery charge

2 kiwifruit, peeled
2 cups seedless green grapes

Juice the kiwifruit flesh with the grapes. Pour the juice into a glass and add some crushed ice. Decorate with kiwifruit, if desired.

Makes about 1¼ cups

kale and hearty

3–4 kale leaves
3½ oz wheatgrass
1 teaspoon spirulina powder

Juice the kale and the wheatgrass, then stir in the spirulina powder. Serve in a small glass decorated with wheatgrass blades.

Makes about 3 tablespoons

juicy lucy

½ watermelon, about ½ lb flesh
1 cup strawberries

Juice the fruit and whizz in a blender with a couple of ice cubes. Serve decorated with mint leaves and whole or sliced strawberries, if desired.

Makes about ¾ cup

battery charge

kale and hearty

juicy lucy

Index of Juices and Smoothies

Index of Ingredients

Acknowledgments

The publisher would like to thank UK Juicers,
29b Mill Lane, Acaster Malbis, York, YO23 2UJ
(tel: 01904 704705) www.ukjuicers.com
for the loan of the Greenstar Juicer.

Executive Editor: Nicola Hill
Editor: Jessica Cowie
Executive Art Editor: Geoff Fennell
Designer: Sue Michniewiz
Production Controller: Viv Cracknell
Photographer: Stephen Conroy
Home Economist: David Morgan
Stylist: Angela Swaffield

Juice recipes written by
Amanda Cross and **Fiona Hunter**

fruit smoothie (see page 18)

smooth operator

3 carrots
2 figs
I orange
**I inch cube fresh ginger root, roughly
chopped**
½ large banana

Place the carrots, figs, orange, and ginger in the juicer, and whizz together. Put the juice into a blender with the banana and 2 ice cubes and process for 20 seconds. Add more ice cubes and decorate with sliced figs, if desired.

Makes about ¾ cup

bugsy banana

I large carrot
I small orange
½ large banana
I dried apricot

Juice the carrot and orange. Whizz in a blender with the banana, apricot, and some ice cubes. Decorate with slices of banana, if desired.

Makes about ¾ cup

apple and blueberry smoothie

2 large apples
¼ lb blueberries, fresh or frozen

Juice the apple, then whizz in a blender with the blueberries. Serve in a tumbler.

Makes about ⅔ cup

super shakey

½ pineapple, about ½ lb
½ parsnip
I carrot
¼ cup soy milk

Juice the pineapple, parsnip, and carrot. Whizz in a blender with the soy milk and a couple of ice cubes. Decorate with pineapple wedges, if desired.

Makes about ¾ cup

cool down (see page 44)

summer breeze (see page 100)

morning dew (see page 88)

Why make your own juices?

Fresh, homemade juices surpass anything you can buy from supermarkets or even health food stores. Bought juices usually contain additives and preservatives, and many don't have much fresh juice in them at all. By making your own, you can choose exactly what ingredients to use, and you have the peace of mind of knowing exactly where they came from. For maximum benefit, drink juices immediately after you've made them as the ingredients deteriorate fast once juiced. If you don't, store leftovers in the refrigerator and consume within 24 hours.

Choosing and preparing ingredients

The quality of a juice is directly related to the freshness of the ingredients. Try to use the best you can get, always choosing those with good color and optimum ripeness. Organic produce is free from chemical residues and, although it's more expensive, devotees swear by the improved taste and juiciness. Organic ingredients need not be peeled, which is desirable as most vitamins and minerals tend to lie just below the surface of fruit and vegetable skins (which is also where pesticide residues collect). Prepare ingredients just before using them so that fewer nutrients are lost through oxidization.

Although fresh is usually best, if fruit and vegetables are frozen soon after picking they can be better than fresh produce that is past its best. Summer fruits—strawberries, blueberries, and raspberries—are a good example. If you use canned fruit, make sure it is in natural juice or water, not syrup. Dried fruits, in particular apricots, prunes, and dates, are a concentrated source of sugars, vitamins, and minerals but soak them overnight to make them easier to puree.

To peel or not to peel

Most enzymes, vitamins, and minerals lie just below the skins of fruits and vegetables, so include them where possible. If you use organic produce, you can leave most skins on, but remember to wash each item thoroughly in warm water first. Generally, it is safer to peel non-organic produce. Always peel avocados, bananas, mangoes, papaya, and pineapple. You can leave the skin on unwaxed citrus fruits if some rind is called for in the recipe, but it is more usual to peel them, or squeeze them in a lemon squeezer. Leave the skin on kiwifruit unless the recipe states otherwise.

Remove pits and seeds

Remove large pits such as those in apricots, avocados, mangoes, peaches, and plums. Many melon seeds are full of juice, so unless instructed otherwise, include them, with the exception of papaya seeds. Apple and citrus seeds may make the juice bitter, so don't put them in.

Other ingredients

Other ingredients such as milk, yogurt, nuts, seeds, and herbal teas make for even more interesting and nutritious drinks. Some recipes contain supplements, which are a concentrated source of essential vitamins and minerals. Spirulina is a form of chlorophyll credited with, among other benefits, halting the signs of aging. It is good in juices but may spoil their color. Energizing wheatgrass is also rich in chlorophyll and boosts immunity.

Be creative

Once you have tried some of these recipes, do not be afraid to experiment with some of your own, but follow these simple guidelines:
- Carrots and apples blend well with almost anything.
- Avoid too many strong-tasting vegetables in one juice.
- If using strong- or bitter-tasting vegetables, dilute and sweeten them with carrot and cucumber.

Juicing equipment

You may already own a lemon squeezer and a food processor or blender, but to make the juices in this book you will also need to invest in a specialist juicer which can separate the juice from the pulp of most fruits and vegetables. When choosing, select one that has a big enough opening for larger fruit and vegetables, and one that comes apart for easy cleaning.

Types of juicer

- **Citrus juicer**: commonly known as the humble lemon squeezer, it's ideal for extracting the juice from lemons, limes, oranges, and grapefruit. Citrus fruits can be peeled (leaving as much pith on as possible) and juiced as other ingredients if you prefer. Citrus juices are highly acidic and are best diluted, either with other juices or water.
- **Centrifugal juicer**: this is the most widely available and affordable of the specialized juicers on the market: ingredients are fed into a rapidly spinning grater which separates the pulp from the juice by centrifugal force.
- **Masticating juicer**: this type is more expensive but gives a higher yield. The ingredients are pulverized and forced through a fine wire mesh to extract the maximum amount of liquid.
- **Food processor or blender**: this works by pureeing ingredients and is used to make smoothies, as well as to mix crushed ice into some juices. Make sure your blender or food processor is strong enough to crush ice; if it is not, you can use ice-cold water instead.

Cleaning your juicer

It is very important to clean your juicer thoroughly every time you use it to prevent bacterial growth on any pulp residues. Look for a machine that dismantles easily; otherwise cleaning it becomes an annoying task and you may be discouraged from using it. Soak the equipment in warm soapy water and use a new toothbrush or nail brush to get into those awkward corners. A solution of one part white vinegar to two parts water will reduce staining and discoloration.

Classic Smoothies